TOXIC PEOPLE

Recognizing and Handling Toxic People
in Your Life

Diana Loera

One morning she woke up different.

Done with trying to figure out who
was with her, against her, or walking down
the middle because they didn't have the
guts to pick a side. She was done with
anything that didn't bring her peace.
She realized that opinions were a dime
a dozen, validation was for parking, and
loyalty wasn't a word but a lifestyle. It
was this day that her life changed. And
not because of a man or a job but because
she realized that life is way too short
to leave the key to your happiness
in someone else's pocket.

This book is dedicated to YOU – let your light shine.

Table of Contents

Welcome

Thank you for purchasing this book.

My name is Diana Loera. I've been writing and doing research as a writer for years. Part of my education over the years includes certification as a Life Coach, Happiness Coach, NLP expert and other life improvement certifications. My goal is to bring transformational and helpful books to your doorstep.

The subject of toxic people is growing – people are taking a look at some relationships, a closer look – and looking for options to handle or move away from some people.

People are now recognizing the term and looking for ways to confirm if a person truly is toxic and if so, what one can do to avoid increasing their own stress level when interacting with a toxic person.

Sometimes, in order to be happier in our lives, we need to make changes, evaluate people and situations, and make decisions. Some of those decisions are easier to make and some are much more difficult.

Age sometimes plays a factor, as well as lifestyle and if one has children at home.

In some cases, someone may be fully miserable in a job but needs the income. Or may be living with a person they think may be toxic but have no idea how to evaluate or proceed.

In this book, we'll walk through the subject of toxic people, typical patterns they have, who they associate with, how to detach from them and how to handle them.

Included in this book is a bonus workbook designed to help you process and reflect different aspect of dealing with a toxic person.

You'll see that I write as though you and I are sitting across from each other, maybe having lunch, at Starbucks or in my office.

This is not a dry textbook style book – we all have a tight time schedule and want quick information – and that is my goal. I provide valuable information that you can quickly use and apply – beginning today.

In this book we will go over toxic people, such as indicators and red flags that show a person could be toxic.

I've included a few stories as examples – you can decide if you want to read them or not, but I will say, they are great examples of how a toxic person can pop up about anywhere.

The workbook included inside this book is made specifically for you. There are no right or wrong answers. Each person's workbook will be different when complete as each person is unique and different and unfortunately, toxic people are not cookie cutter made. Each one is different.

You'll be able to reflect on topics such as how you became involved with this person and when you realized they may be toxic.

Ideally, your reflection and answer will help you recognize a toxic person from before or presently so you can handle or avoid this person and also help you see how you became connected with a toxic person in your life now. Were you vulnerable? Were there red flags? What occurred when you became involved? Questions and your answers to them will help you see any missed warning signs and prepare you to recognize them in your future.

So, with this being said, let's begin.

What are Toxic Situations and How Do You Recognize Them?

Chances are you've already heard the term *toxic people* or *toxic situations.*

Most likely, since you're reading this book, you have a person in mind who you think could be toxic.

Toxic situations are minefields for making one's life miserable while the toxic person skates merrily along like nothing happens.

Quite often, the toxic person is covertly planning his or her next attack. They delight in goading their target.

A top one on the attack list is the cold shoulder/not speaking to their target. It is often highly elevated and designed to make the target feel like they have done something wrong when they haven't done anything. A toxic person's focus is to make their target feel small.

Of course, not every person who gives you the cold shoulder is toxic. Some people just are not good with communicating and sometimes that lack results in avoidance or ignoring someone versus communicating and expressing their feelings.

Toxic is manipulation like nothing you've ever seen before. It leaves you exhausted and wondering if you are actually the problem, not the toxic person – which is exactly what the toxic person wants to occur.

Toxic situations are based in negativity, and they are destructive. They can and will suck you down, destroy your sense of well-being and self-worth. The days will fly by, and you will feel worse and worse.

You may gain weight (or lose weight). You may feel like you are walking through a minefield daily and when your survival skills kick in, and they will – you may find ways to cope or not be in the firing range of the toxic person.

It doesn't take a rocket scientist to realize that something doesn't feel right; however, sometimes it takes a while for it to become clear that a situation is more than just odd - *it's toxic.*

Examples Where Toxic Situations May Occur

While a toxic person can be most anywhere, here are a few places where you may find a toxic person:

- Friendships
- Marriages
- Family relationships
- Extended family
- Stepfamily
- Dating
- Work environments
- Organizations or clubs
- Co-workers
- People you cross paths with occasionally
- Hair / Nail Salon
- Neighbors
- Bosses
- Classmates
- Parents of children your child attends school with

The place where you may cross paths with a toxic person are endless. If it is someone you see rarely, such as someone who also has their hair cut at your favorite salon, you can find a work around – different day or time perhaps.

If it is a family member you only see once a year, you can accept that they are toxic and handle them accordingly on that one day a year.

In some cases, you may have to decide if you want to live with someone who is toxic (or work closely with them) or if you want to move on and close the door on that relationship. Closing the door may take months or even years. Acknowledging to yourself that the person is toxic is the first step.

Clues That a Person is Toxic

- He or she seems to always be at odds with someone
- He or she will often talk about toxic people in his/her own life
- He or she can go from pleasant to accusing/hostile in the blink of an eye- with no warning
- In the morning, when he or she awakes, you find yourself holding your breath as you have no idea if the person will be pleasant or snarling
- Work problems are always due to someone else – never him or her
- He or she may suddenly quit job – most often due to someone else being the one with problem
- Rational attempts to defuse hostility or confusion are spun out of context
- Covert hostility and/or passive aggressive - often leaving you walking on eggshells
- He or she likes to pit people against each other
- You routinely feel emotionally drained due to this person
- You never know what may set this person off
- You feel you are "walking on eggshells" or across a minefield
- You dread certain holidays and events you enjoyed before due to this person now making the day simply unbearable
- You're accused of simply ridiculous things
- You may stop attending family or work events all together- as it is just easier to not go
- When looking back, you realize more often than not, that you are made to feel inferior or stupid or that things that occur are your fault
- You are mocked and/or belittled
- You are gaslighted – often constantly
- The toxic person becomes openly upset or quietly sullen at the drop of a hat
- Not speaking with you often for days on end is a common trait
- Not recognizing your birthday (or other important date)
- Goading/insulting/degrading you – right before you go to sleep, when he/she leaves in morning, right before you have company, right before you have something important you must do

- Making unreasonable demands on your time such as when you have an appointment, are leaving work on Friday or are obviously in the middle of doing something

These are just a few examples – the list is endless. Odds are, you may have recognized several of these examples or they made you think of other similar examples or new examples.

Recognizing Toxic People

I wish we had a way to identify a toxic person instantly such as a big sign hanging over them, so we could keep moving and avoid them but unfortunately, we are sometimes (probably more often than not) reeled in and have no idea of what is really behind a charming social veneer until later.

Recognizing a situation is toxic takes time. Usually, people without specialized training don't recognize the signs immediately.

A toxic person is capable of putting on an act, an act so well- rehearsed, family, friends and others may not believe you.

The challenge is- the sooner you get away from a toxic person the better and having knowledge to be able to assess a toxic situation is crucial.

Being around a toxic person may tailspin in the blink of an eye. The situation may feel confusing and the natural tendency to help, fix a situation, or appease the toxic people seems like a normal course of action.

Many toxic situations may require professional intervention to stop the dysfunction, heal the damage, and move forward. The best thing one can do to be safe is leave a toxic situation before irreparable damage is done.

Learning how to manage toxic situations takes time and specialized training. If you find yourself wondering if you are in a toxic situation, do your best to assess what is happening and create an exit plan as soon as possible.

Staying connected to a toxic person or thinking it will all suddenly work out will only cause more stress and a leopard doesn't change his spots – there will be no change.

There likely won't be an end to the toxicity any time soon. A year changes to ten years in the blink of an eye. Be wise and minimize your exposure.

We will be going over indicators of a toxic person in this book, and we will do so more than once or twice. It isn't redundancy. There are many different signs someone is toxic

– you may pass by dozens of examples – see another list in this book and suddenly – all the pieces fit.

A Toxic Person May Have the Following Characteristics:

He or she speaks only in very broad generalities (statements that give no details). "They say…," "Everybody thinks…," "Everyone knows…" and similar statements are in continual use, particularly when spreading rumors.

For example, he or she may say to you "Nobody likes to go to that store (or restaurant); everybody hates it." When asked "Who is everybody?" he pretends that it is the opinion of numerous people. If one persists for names - it turns out to be that only one person said it and that one person is the toxic person himself.

He or she deals mainly in bad news, critical or hostile remarks, invalidation (making someone seem wrong or less worthy) and general jabs that keep others down, make them fail, etc.

There is no good news or compliment passed along by such a person.

For example, say you were taking a class and learning to paint using watercolors. The toxic person would be likely to make comments about you had made errors and adding you did not have the basic talent and would never be able to paint.

The toxic person continually selects the wrong target (cause of things) for his or her anger.

I've seen this firsthand, and it can be very frightening. As an example, if he trips over a piece of lumber he didn't put away, he may kick or even slam the board and blame you for the reason the board is there (which makes no sense).

If he has a flat tire because he dropped nails on the driveway and didn't clean up his mess – he blames someone else.

He or she cannot finish a project or action. He or she becomes surrounded with incomplete projects, projects done halfway or shabbily and things that were started and never finished.

They have no sense of actually having caused something and so cannot feel any shame or guilt when they have done something wrong. For example, having an affair, physical or emotional – the toxic person is not to blame. Don't be surprised if the spin it and insist you are the one having an affair.

Knowing the Difference Between Toxic and Straightforward People

Some people have a tendency to speak in a very straightforward manner.

They may even have what is sometimes known as "resting bitch face". At first glance they may look sullen, unapproachable or just mean.

Sometimes they speak, they are to the point, may be gruff and/or not say much.

This does not mean they are toxic in any way.

Some people also simply do not communicate well and come across as hostile or even toxic.

Some people are introverted and are uncomfortable talking with people.

Some people talk about themselves a bit more than others as they don't know what else to talk about.

I do think once you are finished reading this book you will see there is a considerable difference between a toxic person and one with poor communication skills or someone who is introverted.

18 Ways to Recognize a Toxic Person in a Couples Relationship

When you finally realize, something is not right in a relationship, alarm bells may begin wildly ringing in your mind – your gut instinct is that something is just not right. Sometimes it is just a persistent thought or feeling in your head, an uneasy feeling – something is wrong.

Following is a list of most common toxic person indicators – these are ugly and common – odds are if you suspect someone is toxic – this may be a quick checklist for you.

1. Dr. Jekyll & Mr. Hyde personality

I listed this one first as it seems to be the most common. You're never quite sure what to expect from them, one day to the next. One moment they may be warm and fuzzy, but the next might produce unwarranted rage and anger toward you.

2. You are blamed incessantly, often ridiculously, even in public

He or she blames you. No matter what, it is your fault.   The accusations are often just insanely ridiculous.   Sometimes to the point, you go out of your way to avoid them as much as possible and refuse go in public with them.

3. You don't feel relaxed around this person – ever

You dread weekends or anytime you are alone with this person. Even out in public, when he or she is putting on a great charade, you are just waiting for the other shoe to drop, and it is an awful feeling.

4. You are exhausted, may feel blue and listless

Sure, many things may cause a feeling of exhaustion, but if you can trace it back to one person who is exhibiting the traits of a toxic person, that's a sure sign of toxicity. When you're depressed, that spills over to your other relationships, work and friendships. The longer the depression lingers, the tougher it is to dig yourself out of your rut.

5. You find yourself making up stories or exaggerating about how wonderful your life is to others due to being embarrassed about the real story

Especially if you've been married before or people had raised eyebrows when you began dating the toxic person. Perhaps you are embarrassed that you stood up for this person and now see his or her true colors. You find it easier to pretend everything is wonderful in your life. It is a self-survival trait and much more common than you would think. This is also applicable to your work life.

6. Family, friends, co-workers, neighbors and/or even people in public, like store clerks, say something or raise their eyebrows due to the behavior of the toxic person

If you feel the need to constantly gush and reinforce how great things are, as mentioned above – this is a red flag.

7. Your friends see things you don't (or choose to ignore)

If people you trust are telling you that you're being abused or are in an ugly situation, then it may be worth giving them a listen.

8. You divulge less and less to your spouse or significant other

Maintaining a separate social circle is healthy, to a point. But when you start building friendships that do not include your spouse or you become defensive and secretive, I'm willing to wager you are doing so due to the problems that surround your partner.

9. You have thought your spouse or significant other is cheating on you and this can also be emotional affairs

Emotional affairs are pretty much the same as a physical one – your partner is committing himself/herself to someone besides you. It is uncomfortable and hurtful.

10. You are always on the defense

If you have to constantly think about how you're going to defend every little part of your life, this is a big red flag.

11. He or she is indifferent or distant when you're trying to communicate

Not paying attention, whether the issue is big or small, is a sign of disrespect.

12. Your partner could care less about household bills or budgets

He or she may go out to eat daily while you bring a bag lunch to work. Along with personal spending – they may give wads of cash to their family members who do or do not live with you. Or insist on paying for everyone's lunch – handout after handout.

They may max out credit cards and/or overdraft bank accounts (blaming you and having a fit when your monthly budget doesn't allow for you to pay off the credit card spending). They may spend wads of cash on new clothes and proceed to hide those clothes from you – yes men also.

13. Feeling of a lack of control

If he or she is controlling your actions, relationships, and all other areas of your life, then you are connected to a toxic bully.

14 He or she passively-aggressively manipulates you, often in childish ways

He or she gives you the cold shoulder – not speaking to you for days.

15. He or she storms out, is an ongoing source of drama

As mentioned before, the toxic person often has a Dr. Jekyll, Mr. Hyde personality. He or she will storm out, often slamming doors. Sometimes carrying on how you can't manage without them. Or they threaten to leave, carrying on about how you'll never find anyone else and how will you pay the bills when they aren't here?

16. He or she has asked for "one more chance" a lot more than one time

If you've confronted them before over toxic behavior and they have broken promises to change, I assure you this is a toxic person with no desire or willingness to change. However, most toxic people scoff when being called out on their actions – you are dealing with a master manipulator.

17. In the beginning especially, you may rationalize his or her bad behavior

When you cave in, you give him/her more rope to push the lack of boundaries even more.

18. You'd rather be anywhere but around this person

Your home should be a place of refuge, and not a place of misery. You should not be one where you feel you are walking on eggshells. You go out of your way to have as little contact as possible with this individual.

Examples of Toxic People

As you progress through this book, you'll be reading several examples of toxic situations.

Names and some details have been changed but these are actual situations and true stories that I've collected while doing research for this book.

You may be tempted to skip over these stories, and if so, that is up to you.

However, the people who shared them with me, felt as I do – hopefully sharing these stories will help others recognize the signs of a toxic person and will begin taking action as soon as possible.

You'll see that toxic people can show up anywhere – friends, work, personal life.

The most important part is to recognize them for what they are. This book was written with this in mind.

Don't beat yourself up for connecting with a toxic person. They tend to have a wonderful social veneer, they often appear as charming, caring, fun people – until the gloves come off – and believe me they do.

Toxic Friendships

When it came to toxic friendships, this story came to mind, and I think it may give you some insight regarding toxic friendships (names have been changed).

Nicole ended the phone call with her friend from the train and breathed a sigh of relief.

She'd spent over thirty minutes on the phone, and she felt worn out after the conversation.

Every time Nicole had tried to share something positive or upbeat, her friend countered with a negative reaction.

The whole call made Nicole wish she'd never answered the call – once again.

And this was just in the morning. Nicole and her friend rode the same commuter train each morning and went their one separate ways on the train platform.

Many days, before lunch, Nicole would see her phone ringing. She knew she shouldn't be taking personal calls at work.

To be honest, for some reason, she felt anxious not to take the call. She even felt anxious that she might be in the washroom or on a call and miss the call. Her stomach churned most mornings with an ugly anticipation.

Sometimes, Nicole found her friend was fun to talk with but most of the time, her friend was upset over how badly she had been treated by someone in the office or some other slight that always seemed to happen daily.

She seemed easily offended and constantly upset regarding her latest drama.

Nicole called me one day last summer after she saw a brief article regarding toxic people and was worried her friend was toxic.

Nicole's stomach had begun rolling when she heard her phone begin to ring while she was at work. Before she was anxious about the call coming in and now, she was just anxious all day. She began dreading going to work and her declining work performance was noticed. She was passed over for a promotion – it was given to a girl who she used to be just like – on point, efficient and cheerful.

She found herself contemplating a new job, one without a commute even though it meant less pay. She had a car payment and student loan payment, and every penny was needed.

She was at her wit's end regarding what she should do and finally began sending out her resume. Ironically, her commuter friend ended up leaving her job and taking a job closer to her own home. She called Nicole a couple times and over the course of a few months, those calls dwindled down to none.

While her situation is not to be taken lightly, you may have a different situation whereas you interact with a possible toxic person more so than Nicole did or you may even be a in a relationship with someone and every fiber of your being has alarm bells ringing as you know   "something" is not quite right in your relationship, but you aren't able to pinpoint it – yet.

Because toxic people are good at distraction, it can be months or years until you realize that a toxic person is negatively affecting you.

Toxic People Take Your Energy

It's common for toxic people to have frequent catastrophes or urgent situations – that really aren't that urgent.

When Jackie realized this, she thought of her now ex-husband.

To him, everything was one big emergency.

He called her at work several times a day, even when he knew she was in meetings.

If she didn't answer her phone, he'd hang up and redial – over and over.

He never gave her advanced warning about things that were coming up so she found herself routinely rushed and stressed.

When it comes to toxic people, there is always a crisis looming. As a result, you feel like you have to be at their beck and call. You are at the effect of whatever they desire.

Such as saying will be there in fifteen minutes and two hours later shows up, and now you are beyond late. Holding dinner for hours only to hear him complain it is overcooked or whatever complaint he comes up with.

You're constantly shifting your schedule to accommodate their latest problem and you feel helpless to change anything.

Jackie's breaking point came when one icy winter day, she was once again, rushing to get out the door as she had a very important meeting with a new client in Chicago. Which her husband was very well aware of.

As she was rushing out the door, he asked her to make more coffee. You read that right. She had her coat on, keys in hand, stressed over a high-level meeting.

Now this may seem so trivial. After all, there's nothing wrong with making someone some coffee.

However, when the "someone" knows you have a schedule, have a meeting and once again, tries to sabotage and manipulate you – there is a problem.

After she had ended her relationship with him, she called me. She said she realized how toxic it had been when afterwards she found she was much more clearly focused, and she slept. Yes, she slept soundly for eight hours each night versus waking every two hours, most times in high anxiety and never feeling fully rested.

She had grown so accustomed to not being able to sleep it took her a few weeks to be able to accept this new change and that feeling rested was now normal.

Jealousy and Twisting of Reality

Another example of enduring a toxic relationship is Dana.

Dana would receive endless texts from her husband any time she went to her doctor, chiropractor, or dentist. She had been going to these medical professionals since her teens.

One time, he accused her of not actually being at the doctor's office and demanded she send a picture of herself in the office (seriously).

Another time, right before bedtime, he accused her of not going to her chiropractor. Insisting he had left work which means he would have had to drive 30 minutes each way and checked the chiropractor's parking lot – and didn't see her car in the lot.

I have no doubt that he didn't leave work – this is how the operate, they try to trip you up. When you are taken back by the lunacy of the accusation, they insist you are guilty.

Dana had a serious back issue and decided it was easier to struggle with the back pain versus deal with her husband's wrath. She began cancelling her appointments.

Her back pain grew worse due to stress. Her husband would mock her back pain and say she was making it up.

He mocked her when she would struggle to bend over or pick something up.

She gained weight as she was unable to move comfortably, exercise was not even a thought.

When a friend bought her a heated massaging back pad, he once again mocked and degraded her.

She learned to live with back pain that was sometimes excruciating. Until one day she finally had enough and told him to get out.

She said she felt she slept comfortably that night for the first time in years. She awoke feeling refreshed and slowly noticed her back pain was diminishing.

She began walking after work and going to her chiropractor. It was like the black thunderclouds vanished and the sun came back out. She was so relieved and wondered how she had hung on so long.

Manipulation is Their Middle Name

The manipulation varies but it is geared towards making you feel inferior and small.

Usually when one does not give in to a toxic person's manipulation, they quickly become sullen, often shouting, and then ultimately storming out – all your fault of course.

Steve's main manipulation tactic, when thwarted, would typically result in him smashing his phone onto the floor and storming out.

Debbie recounted four phones in two years, all fairly new, all much more costly than hers as he refused to purchase a "cheap" phone.

All four with smashed screens.

He would then return a few hours later and want her to go with to the phone store where he would weave an elaborate story about how the phone broke. Debbie was afraid to say she wouldn't go with him as she worried it would result in another tantrum.

The fourth time, the store owner happened to be in. He listened to the elaborate tale and looked hard at Debbie. She knew he saw right through the lies, and she also knew she needed to end this relationship.

Steve may have sensed a change was in the wind as his previous threats of leaving slowed down. Debbie still quietly continued her planning of moving on.

One hot summer night, they had gone out to dinner. On the way home, he began ranting as he wanted her to co-sign on a new sports car and she had refused, saying it was well out of their budget.

He was screaming how she would never find anyone who would put up with her. Instead of begging him to stay, as she had before, she sat quietly. He raged on, running a traffic light and she prayed for a police officer to pull him over, but none were near the intersection. Once home, he shouted, she would see, how bad it was without him and be calling him begging him to come back and he left.

Well, she didn't call. A week later, he returned. The argument was all her fault, according to him but he was willing to give her one more chance.

She didn't want that "one more chance" but she also knew, financially, she needed time to get herself in a better situation.

She continued planning and was ready when a few months later, he had yet another blaming session.

The morning after he stormed out, she made two calls – one to a locksmith to change all locks and the second to an attorney she had already contacted.

A great sense of relief and calm washed over her.

She was done, chapter closed.

Toxic People Swipe Your Time

Toxic people don't respect your time and have no problem taking it when they want to.

It could be the co-worker or boss that expects you to help her with her responsibilities, regardless of how much work you already have on your plate.

The same toxic people that want to take your time usually don't have time to help you when you need it.

They have no problem fiercely guarding their time because they think their time is valuable, which is the exact opposite of how they treat your time.

The important thing to remember when you're dealing with toxic people is that they subtract things from your life.

But in healthy personal and professional relationships, you feel like things are being added to your life – more hope, more energy, and most importantly, more joy.

Mary worked in a medium sized office. She was in charge of HR. Her boss was constantly forcing her to stay over even though her work was done, and she had to pick up her two small children at daycare.

Mary liked her job; the pay was decent and she was fairly close to home and the children's daycare.

The constant toxic actions of her boss were numerous, I'll only share a couple examples.

One day her boss needed copies made – boxes of copies, Mary was working and had file boxes dumped on her desk. She was told her boss wanted copies made immediately. To begin, this wasn't even Mary's job to make copies. She didn't mind helping but advance notice would be appreciated.

She had to drive across town and hand feed the documents (after removing staples) and then reassemble and staple each one. Lunch time came and went as Mary pushed to get the boxes done without a break.

She got back to the office with the boxes. A co-worker pulled her aside and said she had gone to Mary's office with a question regarding HR.

Mary's boss had seen her and asked what she needed. The woman said she would come back as Mary wasn't in her office.

Mary's boss demanded the woman write up a complaint and give it to her (Mary's boss) as Mary wasn't available.

The woman refused to do so. Mary continued on to her office with her heart pounding and stomach churning.

There on her desk was a complaint form, written by her boss, stating Mary wasn't available to answer an HR question for an employee and this served as a formal warning.

Mary went home and cried that night. She needed her job, but this was simply insane. She had a family vacation planned in a couple months and decided to stick it out until she at least had her vacation.

The Friday before her vacation began finally came. At five minutes before 5 when everyone was getting ready to leave for the weekend, Mary's boss buzzed her on her desk phone. She needed her to take something to the post office and send it priority mail.

Mary later told me this woman had taken a two-hour lunch and also walked by her office countless times that day.

In other words, she had plenty time to do this task and once again, it wasn't Mary's job to do it. From the sound of it, she had set this up to intentionally badger Mary.

Mary felt tears welling up, they had hotel reservations and needed get on the road now. The post office was in the opposite direction of her home by a good thirty minutes and her boss also wanted her to return with the receipt from the post office.

A co-worker overheard the conversation and offered to go to the post office. Mary knew this would result in yet another unwarranted write up and she declined the offer.

She had endured two years of the toxic behavior exhibited by this woman. She dreaded Mondays and each week cried at least a couple times on her way home or sometimes in the bathroom at the office.

Mary went to the post office that day. She went on her vacation and began sending out her resume while on vacation.

Before her vacation ended, she had an interview scheduled.

She gave several co-workers names as references and the receptionist made sure the reference calls were smoothly routed without her boss hearing about it.

Mary found out how many friends she had at work and how many people saw how toxic her boss was.

Toxic people come in all shapes and sizes. Some are blatantly obvious, and some are so sly that you may doubt your feeling regarding them being toxic.

Toxic People, Continuing Education and the Workplace

This example happened in an office and while is a longer story – I hope you see how a toxic person can easily operate in a workplace.

Jack worked in a small office. He had solid skills and was actually more skilled than the department head. Above him, going up the office ladder, was a woman who was skilled and did a good job. She was his immediate supervisor. She reported to the department head.

The department head was friends with the business owner, and it was no secret this was how he landed the job.

Jack worked hard and many times he stayed late or came in on the weekend. A year after he began, his immediate supervisor took him aside and said she was going to be giving her resignation soon as she had found a much better job.

Jack was glad for her but also hated seeing her go. She said she was recommending him for her position, he certainly was qualified for it and had the work ethic.

The day came when his supervisor left. The following Monday, he was called in to the office of the department head.

He was handed basically all of his now former supervisor's workload and the keys to her office. Before, he had been in an open area on the floor. It wasn't bad but an office sure would be nice.

I know we all hate to assume but I think it was logical to think he was being promoted and getting an office.

Not so fast – remember, we have a toxic person in the mix.

He was informed he was now on salary.

As the meeting was closing, the department head told Jack to go in the former supervisor's office and move all the files to his area.

I'm sure Jack blinked twice as this certainly wasn't what seemed to be unfolding. Jack said he would do so and paused a second as he realized a promotion wasn't forthcoming.

He looked at the department head and stated he would like to be considered for the now vacant position – and this is where the wheel really fell off the bus and the toxic level went up a notch.

The department head's head snapped up and he looked at Jack in a way Jack said was indescribable – like he was nothing.

He replied "What?" and Jack repeated what he said.

After a long pause, the department head replied Jack was in no way qualified (he absolutely was qualified, and this was the pot calling the kettle black) and he (the department head) would be "holding the position from above" until a "suitable" replacement was found.

In other words – no raise, no title and more work for Jack. He was on salary, but it equaled his current 40 hour a week pay.

Jack was taken aback but figured better to show he was a team player and take on the extra workload as surely it would be short term.

Then – the department head's eyes narrowed, and he began accusing Jack of encouraging the supervisor to leave and how he saw now Jack pushed her out as Jack wanted her job.

Jack said it was like the Twilight Zone. His head was spinning. This was pure nonsense and irrational. Jack denied the accusations. He finally managed to get out of the office and went to move the files.

Well, it turned out the supervisor had done a lot more than the department head realized and not only was he fully out of his league with white collar ability, but he also had a surprise coming. The janitor quit. This would not seem like a big deal except the janitor was a big deal and he gave no notice.

Several sets of washrooms, countless fluorescent bulbs needing changed, vacuuming, dusting, mopping, hauling out trash and much more – it was a full-time job.

Based on the office flow chart, the janitor position also reported to Jack's former supervisor and now with her position empty, yes, the janitor job rolled up – to the department head.

Jack was working at his desk, and he looked up to find the department head glowering at him. Evidently there was no toilet paper in at least one bathroom.

This had zero to do with Jack. It was the department head's job now as the janitor had left.

The keys to the supply closet were slammed down on Jack's desk and the department head stormed off.

Jack did the toilet paper refilling. Again, surely it was temporary.

About a week or so later, Jack was summoned to the department head's office where he was berated as the files were not in locked office.

These were the same files he was told to remove from his supervisor's office and keep at his desk.

One would "assume" perhaps now Jack would be (finally) getting an office. Instead, the files were given their own office and Jack was to remain at his desk.

So, Jack moved the files back all the while feeling like he was in a bad dream.

This is a typical classic trait of a toxic person – they will make you feel like you have done something wrong.

Weeks went by and like a frog in a pot of boiling water, the temperature had slowly been increased and Jack had no idea the water was boiling but it was about to get worse, under the pretense of getting better.

Once again, following the typical toxic person path.

Jack was called in and told to sit. He was grudgingly told; he would be in a new program. He would be "in training" for the job he had wanted before (now he wasn't as thrilled).

I think you know what unfolded – he was handed the job, "in training", and no pay raise. We could say well, this is just an example of a bad boss not a toxic boss but in fact, being toxic is what made him a bad boss.

There was one more part to be revealed. The department head informed Jack he didn't have the skillset needed for the position (he did indeed have it and then some) and he would need to attend classes off site – one day a week on company time (with pay) and one day on the weekend (no additional pay nor would gas or meals be provided either day)

The class was almost a two hour drive each way. The hours were his work hours now. He would need leave two plus hours earlier and get home two plus hours later.

He would also do this on a weekend day.

He was not compensated for gas or food or tolls. If he wanted to be in training for the position, this was what he needed to do.

When we are around a toxic person and entangled in their web, we sometimes do things we never would have dreamed of doing before and after we get out of their web, we wonder how we were so stupid.

It is not due to being gullible or stupid – toxic people are masters of manipulation.

Jack figured a bird in the hand was worth two in the bush. He would have a new title and while he didn't plan on being at this place forever, it would look good on a resume. So, two days a week, he began commuting. The class was basic, really had nothing to do at all with his once desired job but, in due fairness, it got him out of that office once a week, with pay, even though he had forfeited a weekend day.

He often wondered how long it took his boss to even find this course.

Toxic person lesson – they thrive on making obstacles such as this one and Jack unwittingly walked in and soon found the heat turned up as he didn't balk or back talk his boss.

Remember, they thrive on drama and squashing people. Jack going weekly (his day was a Friday, also, I'm sure, well thought out by his boss as he was often stuck in dreaded Friday rush hour traffic) plus he went again on Saturday.

He managed keep everything going smoothly at work, mainly by staying over in the evenings and coming in on Sunday.

He was almost halfway done with the course (it was months long). Once again, he was summoned.

How was the course? Great! Halfway done now. Instead of praise or even acknowledgment, he was informed change in plans. They could no longer send him during week – too hard not having him in office (pure nonsense). Now he had to go only on weekends. He could go one day or both.

Even though it would slow his progress by half, Jack had to go only one day. He needed the second weekend day for handling office work and also, he wanted to spend some time with his family.

Slowly, he finished his course.

No acknowledgment of completion, no news of a raise. The days passed.

Before you think, why didn't he look for work elsewhere? Remember the carrot being dangled.

A few weeks later, he was informed there was another course being held out of state over a weekend. He would need pay for the course, his airfare and meals.

Jack spoke with his wife. Money was tight, he had been commuting for the last course. But surely this meant the promotion was near. They decided to ask Jack's parents if they could loan the money to be paid back asap, even faster once he had the new position.

During all of this chaos, several new people had been hired at the company. One was a waitress from a local diner. Nothing out of the ordinary, but Jack was soon to be thrown an unimaginable curveball – a trademark of toxic people.

He went to the out of state seminar. Had to stay at a low rate but clean motel and use public transportation but he made it work.

Very shortly upon his return, he was informed changes were being made effective immediately.

The waitress now had the position he had been "in training " for. She was a nice young woman, straight out of high school.

She was now dating his boss. She had an office. There was no training – at all.

Jack had two options – work in their call center or be an outside salesman. He chose (smartly) the salesman as he needed look for a new job – fast.

Being out of the building, would make looking for a new job hopefully easier.

He heard from fellow employees what shambles his department quickly became. He was wasting no time – his survival skills were on high alert.

He found another job, making more money and gave his two-week notice.

He was dragged into the company conference room by his boss and by the company owner (who I suspect was also toxic). He said he was pretty sure they recorded the conversation – I am too.

He was berated and belittled – how ungrateful he was. All they had done for him. Typical behavior of toxic people – degrade and belittle. Make you feel small, small, small.

Then he was presented an invoice. Yes, an invoice – for the training he had been forced to do. Seriously.

He had his wits about him enough to be able to spit out the words and say he had paid for gas, meals and the entire out of state training. The owner seemed taken back when he said he had paid and wanted proof.

Well, it just so happened he had copies of his plane ticket, hotel and other bills, showing the end of his debit card number on each one.

This seemed take them back – toxic people who do not see their victims cowering, usually are like a fire with gas poured on – they come out swinging. Except, Jack had proof and as mentioned they were most likely recording him, for whatever reason.

Jack finished the meeting, packed his belongings and left. He was done.

Jack's story was long, thank you for hanging on and reading through it as it is a valuable example of a toxic boss.

A toxic person is threatened by anyone they perceive as better than them. It may be education or even physical looks. But if a toxic person feels threatened, they seek to degrade and if possible, remove the person from their path.

Jack's boss was in no way qualified for the job that he held. Jack was a threat to him as he could have easily held the position his boss held and actually do the job. This cycle will continue with a toxic boss. You may see a high employee turnover or at the least, disgruntled and bitter employees.

The Know-It-All Toxic Person

Nancy had run several large corporations and was a well - respected businesswoman.

Her husband seemed always have a problem with work. He'd last a short time and even was known to abruptly quit his job – never his fault of course.

Nancy, being very solid with finance, thought about possibly opening a business with her husband.

He had bragged incessantly how he had been self - employed before they met and how good his business sense was. His reason for closing his business had made sense at the time. Maybe he needed to have his own business.

As she thought over the idea, she ran the numbers and knew she could comfortably take a leave from working, help her husband set up the business and return to her own business world in a year, two at most.

So, Nancy discussed the idea with her husband and within a few months they were both self-employed.

She rapidly grew their business using the skills she had well-honed over her years in the corporate world.

The problems began cropping up one after the other – her husband wanted to buy this and buy that – with no regard for costs. He wanted hire people when additional help was not needed.

Nancy's stress level climbed. She was working 12-hour days while her husband took 2-hour lunch breaks and simply refused to follow set appointments – instead going to a 4:00pm appointment at 10:00am and not going to another one – at all.

He would amble out the door around 10 each morning, while their competition had been up and moving by 7.

He totally disregarded the day's schedule.

This of course, added a flood of customer calls to Nancy's already hectic day.

She had done all estimates and had great prices for clients plus she had a great profit margin.

Her husband became more and more sullen.

He began giving estimates – blindly.

When she said to him, we're losing money on this job – where are your calculations? He degraded and mocked her – and went on what a good businessperson he was and how stupid she must be because – had he not quoted so low, the client would not have taken the job (you read that right).

He began badmouthing her to customers.   Billing was a nightmare and each month she dreaded sitting down to wade through the mess that laid before her.

One year turned to four – Nancy couldn't hand over the company as she had planned on doing. She couldn't even slip away to get her hair cut as she was beyond overwhelmed due to the chaos around her.

Managing finances was a nightmare as he was spending wildly.

Any time she attempted to discuss the business with her husband, her stomach rolled. When she pushed forward and questioned the lack of organization or unneeded purchases, he would insult her.

He would hire unqualified people demand they be paid managerial rates. Meanwhile, he was now too important to do the labor. Instead he would take two hour lunch breaks and stand around while employees worked.

I spoke with Nancy several times about her ordeal, and she said recognized his toxic behavior. It was like she had lived with a phony before – day and night difference.

In this case, I am fairly certain her husband had a narcissistic personality. Narcissistic people hide their true colors very well.

One day, Nancy went in the office and realized she would never get out from under this nightmare. She decided this would be her last year running the company.

She informed her husband he would need find a job and had a year to do so.

She than began reclaiming her life and her sanity.

As the year rolled to a close, her husband realized his threats and bullying no longer had an effect on her.

He had intentionally snubbed her birthday and their anniversary earlier in the year. He then refused to complete work projects and left clients hanging.

Nancy was fielding angry calls from clients. She watched her company implode and I think as you know, her husband took zero responsibility. Instead, he pointed fingers at her, did nothing for over 4 months and even snubbed her on Christmas, buying not a single gift for her.

He blamed her for the company folding.

In late January, he realized she was serious, and he finally found a low paying job.

Nancy is working on rebuilding her career. Some days are harder than others, but she is determined to succeed. She and her husband parted ways as I'm sure you saw coming.

Toxic People and Your Looks

This may have sounded a bit silly but toxic people often have a button when it comes to how someone else looks. Typically, they make fun of the person on some way or make degrading comments.

Jabs such as:

Your hair style makes you look old.

Weight gain, physical shape, anything they can take a jab at they will.

The outfit you have on looks out of fashion.

Your hand lotion (or other fragrance) smells so overpowering and gives people a headache.

If you leave, no one will want you – for a variety of reasons (a toxic person will tailor this to strike your largest fear).

You've really aged.

Meanwhile, they are primping and preening themselves.

Often, they purchase new clothing for themselves, join a gym or other things, and of course, do not divulge this to you.

Toxic people tear down others to make themselves feel powerful – remember that and let their hateful jabs roll right off of you. Once you've recognized a person is toxic, while the jabs are hateful, you know what you are dealing with, and you are no longer blindsided when snide comments are made. Instead you are now in the catbird seat as you understand what type of person you are dealing with.

They will also tear down your friends and family members. Insulting anyone who makes them feel threatened. This is not physically threatened. They perceive the person as a threat to them, as this person may clue you in to what the toxic person is hiding behind his or her social veneer.

Jealousy

Sharing good news with a toxic person often ends in an argument or in making you feel small or worthless.

Whether your win was big or small, a toxic person always downplays it. If they do acknowledge how hard you worked, they may do so in the form of a backhanded compliment.

An example of a backhanded compliment would be the friend that upon hearing about the new business deal you just closed says, "I'm so happy your little business is finally profitable."

While this comment may sound innocent, the toxic person is clearly trying to downplay your success.

Laughing sarcastically when you are telling someone about your good news is another red flag.

These types of comments and actions usually stem from jealousy and have nothing to do with you.

The solution to handling this type of situation is easy.

Stop sharing good news with people that would rather tear you down versus celebrate with you. You deserve better.

Their Judgment Leaves You Doubting Yourself

Some toxic people might act judgmental or say judgmental things.

This type of behavior can leave you feeling like you must earn approval from the toxic person in your life. You may find yourself censoring not just what you say but who you are. As a result, you feel like you can't be authentic with this person or around them.

Judgement is one of the chief ways that a toxic person stunts your growth.

They don't want you to better yourself or your business. They want to keep you on their level or even slightly below their level.

An example of this might be the client that posts negative testimonials on your website or LinkedIn profile despite the fact that they love your work.

Or a "friend" who makes some odd underhanded jabs at you, usually when in a group.

Don't look to a toxic friend, partner or client for support about a life or business change you're making.

Instead, only tell people that you know will be genuinely happy for you and encourage you.

Their Insecurity Steals Your Spotlight

A toxic person is often insecure.

One of the ways that you'll see this behavior is that they have difficulty sharing the spotlight. They want you to know that however great your life is, theirs is better.

If you've finally received a pay increase, they will carry on how good they are in business.

Buying a new or used car? They will undermine what you bought. Don't be surprised if they buy a model above yours.

I know of one person who had to purchase something one step up from another family member's even something as trivial as a wheelbarrow. Then drive with said purchase to the person's home to show them.

Another example is extreme jealousy over a larger purchase someone makes such as a home or vehicle. The toxic person will seethe and exhibit fully irrational behavior.

No matter how smart you are, how much you make, how much you are valued at work, this person will find a way to undermine or degrade you.

Competition – In a Weird Way

Toxic people change things into competitions.

Toxic family, friends or clients can turn everything into a competition. Even seemingly small things like the number of your social media followers or how much weight you lost can be a source of competition.

The worst thing you can do with this type of toxicity is trying to win. Instead, you should refuse to join in the competition. For example, a friend wants to compare the amount of money you both make.

Instead of naming a dollar amount, say something simple like, "I have enough to pay my bills and I'm grateful for that." This shuts down the toxic person and doesn't give them a way to compare anything.

Understanding why toxic people behave the way they do can make it easier for you to navigate your personal or professional relationship.

However, don't make the mistake of thinking that you can change a toxic person's outlook. If someone is determined to live in negativity and fear with a poor mindset, there's not much you can do to change them. Instead, concentrate on bettering yourself and if possible, limit your time with this toxic person.

Scare Tactics Toxic People Frequently Use

Most likely, if you're reading this book, you are doing so with a specific person in mind.

You look back at your relationship with this person and possibly you have wanted to end the relationship, possibly for years – yet you haven't.

This is absolutely not your fault and is much more common than many people realize.

What keeps you trapped in this web?

The reason isn't because you're weak or that you're a bad person.

The real reason is that toxic people are extremely good when it comes to manipulating others.

Toxic people seek to control you and any and all situations.

They do it so covertly and they do it so smoothly that it's easy to miss the warning signs.

We'll go over the top tactics but remember, everyone is different and even if their tactic isn't listed, it doesn't eliminate them from being toxic. Trust your instinct, you haven't come this far for no reason.

Tactic #1: Intimidation

A toxic person often uses intimidation and fear to control others.

Sometimes, these tactics can be hard to recognize. It might be the veiled threat that a client will badmouth in the industry or that a friend will "accidentally" slip up and share a secret about you with the rest of your community.

Married spouses may hear things like – You'll never make it financially or you'll be alone the rest of your life as no one will want you.

Disparaging comments about weight and age are also common.

Sometimes, the threats aren't veiled, such as the client that says he'll leave a bad review of your services if you don't give him a discount.

The goal of intimidation is to get you to back down. Your best option is to act unaffected. If you show fear or concern, the toxic person may be more likely to follow through with their threat.

Tactic #2: Feigning Innocence

Your significant other made an unkind remark about you hair style or outfit when the two of you are out with another couple.

Odds are the server may have also been standing there so three people have heard this snide comment.

When it is evident you are upset, your significant other brushes you off and says well it was only a joke (and may even use that as more of a reason to invalidate you – that you didn't grasp it was a joke).

When you get offended, your friend acts innocent. She brushes off your hurt feelings and dismisses what she said as "only a joke". Despite your friend's denial, you still feel hurt.

Toxic people will feign innocence when they hurt you.

They reject the idea that you could possibly be upset because no harm was intended—or at least, that's what they'll say.

When it comes to this type of situation, listen to your intuition. If your intuition tells you that the remark was something more, then trust that feeling. If you are right, you'll soon spot more of the same behavior.

Tactic #3: Gaslighting

Toxic people may attempt to gaslight you.

Gaslighting is when a person tries to convince that you're wrong by making you question yourself.

Instead of acknowledging they did anything wrong, they tell you that you didn't see what you thought you saw, you didn't hear what you thought you did and/or refuse to even acknowledge what you have said.

Basically, you are made to feel stupid, like an idiot or even crazy by voicing your opinion.

The phrase originated from a 1938 mystery thriller written by British playwright Patrick Hamilton called Gas Light, made into a popular movie in 1944 starring Ingrid Bergman and Charles Boyer.

In the film, husband Gregory manipulates his adoring, trusting wife Paula into believing she can no longer trust her own perceptions of reality.

In one pivotal scene, Gregory causes the gaslights in the house to flicker by turning them on in the attic of the house.

Yet when Paula asks why the gaslights are flickering, he insists that it's not really happening and that it's all in her mind, causing her to doubt her self-perception.

Hence the term "gaslighting" was born.

If a wife questions her husband about a situation, he may put a look of disbelief on his face and say Are you crazy?

He may even go a step further and tell their neighbor, she said whatever it was while shaking his head and rolling his eyes. This of course, is done in front of her.

Of course, that will make her think twice before saying anything again and also make her question her original thoughts on the matter, despite the fact that her gut is telling her she was right.

This is not just limited to couples. A boss or co-worker could also gaslight you.

Tactic #4: Belittling

Toxic people seem to gravitate towards belittling. Verbally knocking you down, making sure you "know your place" and stay backed in a corner.

Belittling comes in all shapes and sizes. Sometimes it is done right before something special or important to you. Sometimes it is something as simple as allowing you to enjoy something such as a tv show as you'll read about next.

Lisa rarely watches TV but there is one show on weekly at 8pm that she really enjoys.

Her boyfriend has belittled her viewing choice weekly. Often talking while he sees she is watching it. Watching videos on his laptop (with the volume up as loudly as possible), getting up and down and basically causing disruptions the entire hour.

During this time, he makes sure to get a few jabs in about what a stupid program it is and why does she need watch it?

He normally comes home and flops down to watch TV each evening after work and also the entire weekend. She has no other show she watches. His shows are often ones she doesn't like but she respects his choices and sits for hours while he watches his shows.

This is just one action among many that put him on her radar as being toxic.

His latest toxic tactic is making sure to be "running late" conveniently coming in a few minutes before her program begins or a few minutes into the show and of course, ready for supper. Or needing a work jacket washed – right then as it needs go in dryer afterwards.

Before you think is a coincidence, on weeks when reruns are on, you can see the wind goes out of his sails. Especially if she has another channel on. His behavior is planned.

She has been planning to move him out of her life for a few months once she recognized he is a toxic person.

A month ago, she received a significant raise at work which she decided not to mention to him. They have separate bank accounts as she noticed he spends wildly, maxing out several credit cards since she's lived with him.

Recently he began belittling her regarding how he makes more money than she does, despite her having a college education. The belittling is constant and unfounded. By the way, her recent raise has her making considerably more than he does but she wasn't going to volunteer that information.

Belittling comes in all shapes and sizes. It may be a jab, or it may be a steady flood of comments.

There is never recognition for things accomplished. There is always a better idea, better route, no matter what, the toxic person makes sure to invalidate.

Tactic #5: Degrading and Accusations

Degrading comes in all shapes and sizes. Most times a toxic person will do this away from others so not to tarnish the wholesome picture of himself/herself he has painted.

The basis of degrading is to make you feel small and unworthy.

Accusations are often wildly bizarre. Such as accusing of having an affair with your doctor or not being a work or whatever – they are off the rails.

Tactic #6: Verbal and/or Physical Abuse

Physical abuse is a whole new ballgame – if you are being physically abused, find someone to help you immediately.

Abuse is not something that will go away by itself.

I'm pretty confident at least one of the above traits made your heart jump or stomach roll as you recognized that trait in the person you have had in mind.

I'll add something also – Narcissistic. I am pretty confident this person has narcissistic tendencies also.

A toxic person will use everything they know about you to make you doubt yourself.

For example, a toxic person might tell you that you doubt their intentions because you had a bad childhood and don't know what real love looks like.

A client might tell you that he won't offer you more lucrative projects because you just aren't ready yet.

Don't feel bad if you've missed some of the signs that your family member, friend or client is a toxic person.

Now that you know, you can confront the truth and decide what to do.

Whatever your choice, you don't have to apologize for it.

You deserve good relationships in your life.

How to Handle Toxic People in Your Life Using Boundaries

Toxic people can be found in any area of your life.

But just because you're collaborating with that toxic business partner or living with your toxic spouse doesn't mean you have to accept their toxicity.

You can learn how to handle these toxic people so that you limit the effects they have on your life and business.

Set firm boundaries.

Boundaries allow you to function at your best in both business and life. It can be hard to set them and even harder to stick with them, but boundaries are a necessity when you're dealing with toxic people.

Maybe you have that client that wants to stay in constant communication with you—even during the wee hours of the morning.

This is where setting boundaries can be helpful.

Let your client know (in writing) what your office hours are and when he can expect a response from you.

Let your spouse know it is not okay to call you incessantly at work. You are at work, you are working.

In the workbook at the end of this book, you will have a couple exercises regarding boundaries.

Control is the Key

Control the Conversation

You can't always avoid toxic people. Sometimes, they're a part of your life whether you want them to be or not. If you have to interact with a toxic person, try to stay in control of the conversation. When the conversation takes a bad turn, redirect it.

For example, if your friend always complains each and every time you have lunch together, then you don't want to offer advice or a solution to the problem. Instead, validate her complaints by saying something supportive then redirect the conversation to another topic.

Don't React

In some situations, a toxic person may say or do certain things to provoke a reaction from you. Toxic people rely on pushing your buttons to get the results they want. If you don't give a reaction, they think the button is broken and eventually move on.

Once you start doing this, you must do it every time. If it takes a toxic person saying something obnoxious ten times to get a reaction from you, then next time they want that reaction they'll push your button ten times in a row.

Never Escalate

Toxic clients or friends will try to escalate common everyday situations. They'll escalate the incident until it's a drama so big it's worthy of a theater audience. Doing this makes the toxic person feel validated and they may use this as their typical response to problems in your relationship.

Fortunately, you can prevent dramas like this by refusing to engage.

If the toxic person in your life says or does something annoying, try a neutral response like, "Sounds interesting" or "I hear you". Responses like this make it harder for the toxic person to cause a big scene.

Handling toxic people in your life and your business is tough – control is key.

Toxic Relationships Come in Many Forms

Toxic relationships come in many forms – a client or boss that verbally abused you, a friend that always puts you down, or a significant other that habitually ignores your boundaries.

These relationships, even if you recognize that they aren't healthy, are sometimes difficult to let go of.

But if you want to reclaim your power and truly heal from a toxic relationship, you have to be willing to ask yourself some tough questions. Are you ready? We will also go over some of these questions in the workbook so don't feel you need to dwell on questions now. This is just to begin your thought process before you write down details in your workbook.

What Attracted Me to This Person?

It doesn't matter if this person was a business partner, significant other, or close friend. You chose to allow this person into your life because you found something desirable about him or her.

Maybe you liked the way that your boyfriend made all of the decisions because it made you feel safe and cared for.

Maybe you worked with a business partner because you admired her work ethic and found her attention boosted your low self-confidence.

What Were the Early Warning Signs I Missed?

Most toxic people don't wake up one day and decide to be toxic toward you.

The truth is they've usually been toxic to you since the very beginning. You just didn't notice until six, twelve, or eighteen months down the road. In looking back, now you may see their were warning signs earlier in the relationship.

You have to understand this question is not about assigning self-blame.

It's not your fault that this toxic person was verbally abusive towards you.

However, if you don't examine the warning signs then you'll have left this unhealthy relationship only to be at risk of entering into a relationship with another toxic person.

You can, through no fault of your own, fall into a pattern where you choose friends, business partners, and lovers that are toxic unless you start learning from these experiences.

Maybe the early warning sign was that your significant other was a bit too possessive and didn't want you to have any male friends.

Maybe the early warning sign was that a business partner always gave vague responses and never answered a question directly.

Why Did I Stay with This Person?

There are endless reasons why you stayed as each situation is different.

Just as important as it is to recognize the early warning signs of a toxic person, it's also important to understand why you continued in the relationship.

Some people stay in toxic relationships because they don't want to be alone.

Some people worry about what a potential breakup might do to their reputation or how it will disappoint their loved ones.

Others stayed because they worried, they weren't strong enough to make it on their own.

Having children, being a stay-at-home parent, thinking you'll wait a bit – a bit turns into a year and a year turns into five.

What matters most is you are now looking at this situation – square in the eye – and today is your turning point.

How Can I Use this Experience to Grow?

Once you've analyzed your relationship, it's time to learn from it.

Keep in mind this isn't about indulging in self-guilt or heaping shame on yourself.

It's about using this relationship to grow personally and professionally.

Maybe you learned to trust your own instincts or to be your own best friend.

Whatever you learned, carry that truth with you and don't let anyone take it from you.

Healing from a toxic person is challenging, even on the best of days. Sometimes, it may feel like you take one step forward and two steps backward.

That's part of the healing process. Be patient with yourself during this time and reach out to a trusted friend or family if you feel you need support during your journey.

You may also want to consider a life coach or therapist.

Reaching out for help and moral support is often the steppingstone needed for healing.

Is it Me? How to Identify if Someone is Toxic

One of the hardest issues in the beginning of a toxic relationship is determining if the situation actually is toxic.

Often there are small red flags, easy enough to dismiss during the newness of a relationship.

When we are growing up, we are taught stranger danger. We are taught that there are bad people out there who want to do us harm.

We imagine that these people are obvious and look shady – just like we learned as kids.

The fact is, sometimes the most toxic nasty people look very ordinary and have positions of authority. Recognizing someone is toxic can be difficult without a solid grasp of the topic.

This can leave people feeling like maybe they are overreacting or even toxic themselves when it isn't them.

Toxic people are very clever, and this is an understatement. You probably know this firsthand yourself as you most likely had someone in mind when you began reading this book.

Toxic people have spent years building up to the toxic personality you now see. Most likely they have made their way through life manipulating, bullying, whining, and crying their way to whatever it is they want. They do it for a myriad of reasons and they do it because it works.

Safeguarding Yourself from Toxic People

How does the average person safeguard themselves from toxic people? Below are some steps to follow.

Check out their history:

Long history of broken relationships- Toxic people have a long history of broken relationships. Going as far back as they can remember, they have stories of friendships ending abruptly or on bad terms. They are often at odds with family members and highly judgmental of people they barely know.

Erratic employment history- Toxic people have a hard time with employment. Generally, they have difficulty with authority or maybe a chronic personnel issue. Most likely, they do not have long periods of employment with one company.

Often refer to themselves as a victim or misunderstood- Toxic people often dismiss their unfavorable outcomes as being a victim or misunderstood. Toxic people spend a lot of time focused on the behavior of others rather than their own. They see their negative behavior as justifiable under the circumstances.

Require an abundance of support or affirmation- Toxic people come across as very confident, but this is not true. They generally require a lot of emotional support, which is draining to those around them. Their insecurity is manifested by being highly critical of others while expecting high levels of engagement and sympathy for their needs.

Lies From small to full blown whoppers, toxic people tend to exaggerate, alter facts to worsen (they are always the victim)

Degrading Toxic people degrade others consistently. He or she is always superior.

Choosing the wrong target A toxic person blames others – constantly. He or she is never at fault.

Anger There is an anger simmering – often well-hidden but it is there. It often comes out in unexpected ways. An example – he stumbles over a board, instead moving board, he picks it up and bangs on ground. Tosses right back down versus putting away. Screaming at someone in traffic.

Pay attention to these aspects of toxic people:

They aren't always toxic- One of the reasons it is hard to determine if someone is toxic right off the bat is that their behavior is erratic. They aren't always toxic. Sometimes toxic people can be caring, engaging, and pleasant. Time must pass, and the patterns must reveal themselves, before most people realize how difficult they are.

They carry their authority well- Toxic people are very confident in their stand on everything. They generally believe they are doing the best that they can and have a rational explanation for their bizarre behaviors.

They use gas lighting as a tactic- Gas lighting is a psychological form of manipulation where the victim is made to feel like they are going crazy due to the actions of a toxic person. Gas lighting leaves victims apologizing and modifying their own behavior at the beck and call of the toxic person - in very unhealthy ways.

If you have identified someone as toxic, it is important that you take steps to keep your sanity and your safety. While not all toxic people are dangerous, all toxic people have the potential to undermine and impact others in big ways. Do what you must to redefine the relationship and keep yourself at arm's length from the toxic person.

Narcissistic and Toxic Go Hand in Hand

I've been asked more than a few times, if I think a person is narcissistic and/or toxic.

Usually, the person asking the question has focused on the person being one or the other. I firmly believe, these go hand in hand.

In my opinion, narcissistic may be what is spotted first but usually, it takes some time before one really begins to notice the narcissistic behavior and a much longer time before one pegs a person as a possible narcistic person.

A narcissistic person someone who inflated sense of their own importance. They crave and demand attention and admiration (excessively).

This is much more than the average person who liked to be recognized for effort put in or work done. This is a train wreck of a manipulator, carefully concealed.

This also leagues above what may be a conceited or vain person.

They usually have a path behind them strewn with troubled relationships, arguments, fights and other non-optimum relationship issues. They also cover this path extremely well but when you uncover it, it can be extreme and jarring.

Narcissism is a mental condition and can be dangerous.

The odds are quite high that narcissistic person is toxic. A toxic person may not necessarily be a narcissist.

How Toxic Situations Hurt Everyone Involved

It seems understandable that a toxic situation hurts the people being infected and affected by the toxicity, but it may surprise you to know that toxic situation hurt everyone *whether they know it or not.*

Let's look at the obvious.

Toxic situations hurt victims- Those who are subjected to the unrest and negativity are the most vulnerable and likely to suffer. Here are some scenarios:

In the home: Family members who live with toxic people tend to suffer from depression, weight gain, anxiety, apathy, and much more. They may have physical and mental health issues as a result of the negativity and bullying that they live with day-to-day.

At work: Employees and co-workers who are forced to co-exist with toxic people have a higher rate of absenteeism, businesses have a high rate of turn over, and overall morale is generally lower, causing low productivity.

In Friendships: Friends who continue toxic relationships may bring their anxieties home. Unaware or unable to understand the impact their toxic friendship is having on them, they may have angry outbursts or other uncontrolled emotions that leak out when they should be enjoying their family time.

In each of these situations, being subjected to toxic people or toxic cultures can cause a multitude of problems from mental to physical and takes a toll on livelihood and general well-being.

While most people would agree that this toxicity hurts those subjected to the poison, they may not see the impact it is having on the perpetrators as well. When toxic situations and/or toxic people are not held accountable, all parties become contributors to the problem. There is no longer a line between villain and victim.

Let's look at the not so obvious.

Toxic situations hurt perpetrators- Those at the root of the problem dishing out the toxicity are also being negatively impacted by their own behaviors. Here are some scenarios:

In the home: People who bully, play the victim, and demand unreasonable amounts of attention are creating dynamics that they fear the most. Generally, people who operate in dysfunction are coming from a place of fear. They often bring the things they fear most- alienation, distrust, abandonment- into their lives themselves.

At work: From management down, toxic employees drive away good people. If a business owner is toxic, they likely won't have staff long enough to make a profit. If a toxic employee is not managed or eliminated, they can not only cause productivity to diminish, they can cause lawsuits brought on by affected employees or disgruntled customers.

In friendships: Toxic friends who do not face their demons can find themselves at risk of being abandoned or, at the very least, subjects of gossip and fodder. Men and women who lack awareness or accept responsibility for their destructive behavior can be at risk of dangerous self-harm or outward harm towards others.

So, why do people remain toxic and/or remain in toxic situations? Frankly, toxic people are oftentimes in authority and resist being called out on their behavior. The risk isn't worth the reward to the victims and the price of change isn't low enough to the perpetrator, so the cycle goes on and on.

The best thing for all in involved is requiring that perpetrators be held accountable, and victims require health above all else - in all situations and at all costs. Toxic situations hurt everyone involved and must be managed for the health and welfare of the group as a whole.

Getting in the Catbird Seat – How to Handle Toxic People with Calmness, Control and Power

We've covered quite a bit thus far. Some topics, we've gone over more than once. Now we're to the point where we need to put you in the catbird seat.

When you begin using these power tips, I'd like you to remember – YOU are sitting in the catbird seat now.

The term sitting in the catbird seat originated in the Southern USA and was popularized by a sports announcer named Red Barber.

Red Barber called baseball games in the 1930s through the 1960s, and often used American idioms in his play-by-play broadcasts.

When one is in the catbird seat they are in a position where they have the upper hand, best advantage, they are in the power seat.

The phrase originated from seeing a catbird perched up high on corn stalks, bushes etc. He can see over the tops of everything – his perch is enviable, and he is at a great advantage.

So, here we go – let's put you in that catbird seat.

Understand What You Are Dealing With

Call a spade a spade. Toxic people are all around you. You cross paths on the train, at the grocery, online, and other places.

The challenge comes when you need to deal with the toxic person daily such as in a work environment or relationship.

Recognize the person is toxic and that you will be in control of all situations regarding dealing with the person.

Accept responsibility for making the change – to protect yourself mentally and possibly physically.

Again – if you are the victim of physical abuse, stop reading right now and call someone for help. Be it a trusted family member, friend, attorney, hotline or law enforcement. Physical abuse is not okay.

Take Responsibility

If it is going to be – it is up to me. We've all heard that phrase. Today, you are going to claim it. You are a victim no longer. You have confidence, knowledge and you are going to handle this matter.

The Past is Behind You

No more complaining to friends, family or whoever else. You are moving forward – beginning right now.

Responding to a Toxic Person

When you respond, remember all you've read and learned. Respond with confidence. Don't take the bait.

A toxic person knows your triggers. He or she knows how to push your buttons. Think about your triggers – what is it that really rattles you?

It isn't going to anymore. It may take a few times, but you will become unrattled.

You do not have to raise your voice, swear or be rude.

In your mind, take a step back. Recognize the toxic trap that lies before you. This may not be easy the first couple times as these jabs most likely rattle you emotionally.

But beginning today, you are going to recognize them for what they are – attempts to provoke and rattle you.

And beginning today – they no longer work.

Some people imagine a shield around them, bouncing the toxic comments right off of them. Some people imagine a favorite place or moment. Some people recognize the toxic person's hold on them is now over.

You will be rattling the cage when you have this shift from victim to confidence.

The toxic person may attempt to rattle you even more. Remember all you've learned.

Boundaries In Place

Last but not least, being in the catbird seat means you have boundaries in place.

Just a few examples of what boundaries in place will stop -

No more dropping what you are doing to appease a toxic person.

It is fine for someone to ask you to do something. But no means no.

It is fine for someone to get the mail but opening your mail – is not acceptable.

Tips for Leaving a Toxic Situation

Wanting to leave a toxic situation is the easiest part. Knowing how and taking the steps is the hardest. Many people stay in bad situations for too long. Leaving can be overwhelming. Days turn into weeks and weeks into days.

Life happens – you may tell yourself you'll wait until after the holidays or until school is out for the summer. Those times come and pass and you are still where you were. It is okay – that is the past.

Now you are moving forward.

Before a toxic situation becomes out of hand, getting out is the best course of action.

Here are five tips for leaving a toxic situation and maintaining your sanity along the way:

Tell someone- Telling someone that you need to leave a bad situation can free up some of the anxiety that comes from the worry associated with the situation. No longer suffering in silence is a good way to make change. From leaving a bad relationship to exiting a toxic career, telling someone will make a difference.

Prepare yourself mentally- People tend to stay in toxic situations far too long. In doing so, the feelings and behaviors that come with the toxicity start to feel normal and familiar. Leaving may feel harder than staying - even though it's the best thing to do. Prepare yourself mentally for the reality that leaving will be hard but staying will be lethal for your spirit.

Get counseling, coaching, or mentoring- Making a big change in your relationships can be overwhelming. You may need the expertise and support of a trained professional. Consult someone or work together with someone who can give you sound advice to make a clean break.

Don't fairytale the situation- Leaving is often easier than being gone. Once a break happens, the impact can diminish, and you may start to forget how intense things were. This can cause you to regret or rethink your position. Don't fairytale the significance that a toxic situation has once you have removed yourself from harm's way.

Take a break- Recovering from toxic relationships is important. Do what you need to do for self-care and healing. From counseling, to taking a vacation to clear your head, do what you need to do to refresh, regroup, and recalibrate.

Breaking free from toxic relationships and situations is not for the faint of heart. These tips are a solid way to learn, take action and make the changes that are needed to live a healthy life. You don't have to suffer, you don't have to diminish yourself, and you don't have to stay when the right thing to do is go.

Preparing for Change

Keep a logbook – dates, places, time – describe situation with no emotions. A logbook will prove invaluable later.

You'll have a paper trail of consistent examples for use during a divorce or split such as spending and bills.

There is not a specific strategy on how to leave a toxic situation. Each person is different and your plan may be totally different than you expected.

Some people are able to walk away a lot easier than others. Much of this depends on you and the nature of your relationship with your spouse, significant other or workplace.

But there are some general guidelines to consider, no matter what your situation is.

The biggest battle is going to be the one that is fought in your mind.

You have to not only want to leave a toxic relationship, but you also have to set a goal (meaning a specific date) to make your break.

That can take time or perhaps not.

You'll need to plan for how to take care of yourself, and that could require going back to school, getting a better job, or doing whatever it takes to achieve enough financial independence.

If you have a specialized career, it may take longer to find a new place of employment. You may need to consider relocation.

The main thing is – to begin. Begin looking at options, begin looking at finances and planning a strategy.

Even if you give yourself a 6 month exit plan, if you needed to find a new job and haven't, keep working on the plan, it may be 7 months or a year, but you have a plan and are working hard to make it all fall in place.

Recovering From and Guarding Against New Toxic Situations

Once a toxic person is in your rear-view mirror, you'll most likely feel a huge sense of relief.

You may sleep better, not have stomach aches any longer and just feel more alive.

Being suppressed by a toxic person is traumatic.

Once you've managed to remove yourself from a toxic person or situation, it may take a bit of time to get back to being you.

Consider the fact that you may need to consider counseling.

Depending upon your situation you may have PTSD (Post Traumatic Stress Disorder).

Physical issues can include weight loss or weight gain.

You may have experienced emotional overload that resulted in poor eating choices - too much or too little food or the wrong sorts of foods. This may have created problems that remain even after the toxicity is gone. Remember to be kind to yourself. It took time to get this point and it may take time to reset yourself to your ideal weight.

Remember to guard yourself from future toxic situations. Once you've navigated through a toxic encounter, you do have the advantage of knowledge and understanding so you can be alert for red flags.

You'll go through a healing process. It will take time, but you've made it through, no matter how bad it was, you are standing in the light at the end of the tunnel now. Give yourself credit.

Recognizing and Handling Toxic People in Your Life Workbook

We've now reached the workbook section of this book.

Please remember – this is your personal workbook. There are no right or wrong answers.

I set up this section so you will have plenty of writing room (and this is why I published this book in a larger 8 ½ x 11 size).

I hope you take time to reflect on each question.

Now, it's time to dig deep and learn more about yourself.

Try to find a quiet place so you can spend some time reflecting on the questions. Share your honest thoughts here – there's no judgement or right answer.

If at any time you feel overwhelmed or stressed while going through this workbook section, it is okay to set your book aside. If possible, if you can reflect on why a certain question made you feel this way, it may give you some insight that has been hidden on the matter.

You are also free to journal, brainstorm and doodle in this space. Sometimes that random doodling may also bring a thought to mind as you go through your workbook.

Past the questions part of this book, you'll find several blank pages for drawing, doodling, recording notes, examples, experiences – whatever you wish to put on paper. The notes section also is handy for reflections you may have while working your way through questions in the workbook section.

You will decide the pace of doing the workbook. You may want to revisit questions, revise answers, or add to them or change things – totally fine to do.

When I think of a specific person that I know or suspect may be toxic, what specific feeling comes to mind?

When I think of this specific person that I know or suspect may be toxic, what specific memory comes to mind?

Thinking back, what attracted me to the toxic person in my life? Was it something they did or said?

Am I able to be myself with this person? Do I feel accepted by him/her?

Is this person critical or judgmental of me? If so, give an example of this occurring.

Does the relationship provide an even give-and-take exchange of energy? Explain in detail.

Do I feel upbeat and energized when I'm around this person, or depleted and drained? Explain in detail.

Does this person share my values? My level of integrity? Explain in detail.

Is this person committed to our relationship? Why or why not? Give examples.

Can this person celebrate my success or is there one upmanship or jealousy instead? Explain in detail.

Do I feel good about myself when I'm with this person? Why or why not?

Name one or more ways this person has taken up my time or energy in a negative manner.

Do I not share details about certain activities or tasks (such as praise at work or an office Christmas party) because I'm worried how a toxic person in my life will react? If yes, how does this make me feel physically and mentally?

Do I put off certain activities or tasks because I'm worried how a person in my life will react?

If yes, how does this make me feel physically and mentally?

Now, I'll recall a certain person that's always stealing my spotlight, making himself/herself the center of a situation, take credit for things I've done, or in some other way downplaying my work/ability considerably while preening themselves. What are some ways they do this?

Recall someone who used intimidation to "keep you in your place". Did I stand up for myself or back down? Why?

How has this person made me question, second guess or doubt myself?

Does this person make me feel unworthy, ugly or unlovable? Explain in detail.

Imagine my life without this person. What would that look like? Would I be happier, have more energy, see my friends – what would my life be like?

Was I in a vulnerable position at the time I met this person? If so, why?

When did I first begin to get the feeling this person had issues? What did I do at that time?

2. How does this person show a lack of respect towards me?

What have I learned from this toxic relationship?

How can I use this experience to grow?

List an area in my life where I know I need to set some boundaries.

When I think of setting boundaries, how do I feel (anxious, excited, scared, etc.)?

Now, I'll put the boundaries that I want to set in writing. Doing this exercise makes it harder for me to ignore it when someone tries to overstep or trample them.

I've come a long way in my journey. I am confident and informed. How will I use my knowledge to improve myself?

My Notes and Thoughts

My Notes and Thoughts

My Notes and Thoughts

My Notes and Thoughts

My Notes and Thoughts

Closing

I truly hope this book has helped you recognize and handle toxic people in your life. Moving forward may sometimes be a struggle but keep in mind, no matter how slowly you go – you are moving forward, and you've got this!

Wishing you the very best – you deserve it!

Sincerely,

Diana